WEIGHT WATCHERS INSTANT POT FREESTYLE COOKBOOK

BY DR. NAOMI BROWN

CONTENTS

CHAPTER 1: WEIGHT WATCHERS FREESTYLE DIET

Introduction of Zero Points Foods

The diet has introduced more than 200 foods in its zero Freestyle point category. These foods can be consumed without worrying about its nutritional composition. Popular foods with zero points are.

- Beans

- Grapes
- Garlic
- Fresh veggies (limited consumption of avocado, potatoes, olives, and sweet potatoes)
- Lentils
- Lemons
- Most green veggies such as spinach, lettuce, etc.
- Berries
- All bean types
- Turkey breasts
- Chicken breasts
- Egg whites
- All fish types
- Non-fat yogurts
- Fresh fruits or canned fruits (without added sugar)
- Mushrooms
- Tofu
- Okra
- Broccoli
- Bananas
- Asparagus

FOODS TO AVOID

Foods that are completely unhealthy for our body and leads to unwanted weight gains are not recommended in the Weight Watchers programme. Unhealthy foods that are high in bad carbohydrates, saturated fats, and empty calories are avoided in the diet. Foods to avoid while following the diet are:

- Processed meats
- Cakes, cookies, crackers, etc.
- Sugar based commercial drinks and fruit juices
- Potato chips and other commercially fried foods
- Commercial fast foods and cadies

Chapter 2: Breakfast Recipes

Oats Apple Breakfast Cake

Prep Time: 8-10 min.

Cooking Time: 30 min.

Number of Servings: 7-8

SmartPoints: 4

Ingredients:

- 1 cup oats
- 2 cups flour, whole wheat or all purpose

- ½ cup stevia granular or raw honey
- ¼ tsp. salt
- 2 cups, diced apples
- ½ cup applesauce
- ½ cup almond milk
- 1 tsp. vanilla extract
- ¼ tsp. baking soda
- 2 tsps. cinnamon

Directions:

1. In a mixing bowl (heat-proof), mix all the mentioned ingredients.
2. Take an Instant Pot; open the top lid.
3. Pour 1 cup water and place steamer basket/trivet inside the cooking pot.
4. Arrange the bowl over the basket/trivet.
5. Close the top lid and make sure the valve is sealed.
6. Press "MANUAL" cooking function. Adjust cooking time to 20-25 minutes.
7. Allow pressure to build and cook the ingredients for the set time.
8. After the set cooking time ends, press "CANCEL" and then press "NPR". Instant Pot will slowly and naturally release the pressure for 8-10 minutes.
9. Open the top lid, add the cooked mixture in serving plates.
10. Serve warm.

Nutritional Values (Per Serving):

Calories - 164

Fat – 4.5g

Carbohydrates – 32g

Fiber – 4g

Sodium – 104mg

Protein – 3g

Cheese Tomato Omelet

Prep Time: 8-10 min.

Cooking Time: 9 min.

Number of Servings: 5-6

SmartPoints: 4

Ingredients:

- 4 tablespoons tomato paste
- 1 teaspoon salt
- 5 eggs
- ½ cup milk
- 1 tablespoon turmeric
- ½ cup cilantro, minced
- 1 tablespoon butter
- 4 ounces Parmesan cheese, shredded

Directions:

1. Whisk the eggs with the milk and tomato paste in the mixing bowl. Mix in the salt and turmeric.
2. Mix in the cheese and cilantro.
3. Take an Instant Pot; open the top lid.
4. Press "SAUTÉ" cooking function.
5. In the cooking pot area, add the butter and melt it.
6. Add in the egg mixture and spread it to make a round shape.
7. Close the top lid and make sure the valve is sealed.
8. Press "STEAM" cooking function. Adjust cooking time to 8 minutes.
9. Allow pressure to build and cook the ingredients for the set time.
10. After the set cooking time ends, press "CANCEL" and then press "QPR". Instant Pot will quickly release pressure.
11. Open the top lid, add the cooked mixture in serving plates.
12. Serve warm.

Nutritional Values (Per Serving):

Calories - 227

Fat – 14g

Carbohydrates – 7g

Fiber – 1g

Sodium - 374mg

Protein – 14.5g

Ham Egg Frittata

Prep Time: 8-10 min.

Cooking Time: 10 min.

Number of Servings: 4-6

SmartPoints: 2

Ingredients:

- 8 ounces ham, chopped
- 1 teaspoon white pepper
- 1 tablespoon lemon zest
- 1 teaspoon olive oil
- 1 teaspoon salt
- ½ teaspoon paprika
- ½ cup parsley, chopped
- 7 eggs
- ½ cup milk
- 1 tomato, chopped

Directions:

1. Beat the eggs in the mixing bowl. Mix in the milk, salt, paprika, white pepper, and lemon zest.
2. Blend the mix in a blender. Mix in the ham and tomatoes.
3. Take an Instant Pot; open the top lid.
4. Coat the pot using cooking oil. Add the ham mix in the cooking pot. Top with the parsley.
5. Close the top lid and make sure the valve is sealed.
6. Press "STEAM" cooking function. Adjust cooking time to 10 minutes.
7. Allow pressure to build and cook the ingredients for the set time.
8. After the set cooking time ends, press "CANCEL" and then press "QPR". Instant Pot will quickly release pressure.
9. Open the top lid, add the cooked mixture in serving plates.
10. Serve warm.

Nutritional Values (Per Serving):

Calories - 215

Fat – 13g

Carbohydrates – 6.5g

Fiber – 1g

Sodium - 346mg

Protein – 17.5g

Berry Banana Pancakes

Prep Time: 8-10 min.

Cooking Time: 5 min.

Number of Servings: 2

Freestyle Points per Serving: 1

Ingredients:

- 1 teaspoon baking powder
- 1 banana, mashed well
- ¼ teaspoon cinnamon
- 1 teaspoon vanilla
- 2 egg whites

Directions:

1. Take a skillet or saucepan (medium size preferable); heat it over medium cooking flame.
2. Take a mixing bowl (either medium or large size), crack and whisk the egg whites.
3. Stir in the cinnamon, vanilla, and baking powder.
4. Add the banana and mix; divide batter into 4 parts.
5. Add the batter, spread to make round and cook for 2 minutes, flip and cook for 30-45 seconds more.
6. Repeat process for remaining batter. Serve with fresh berries.

Nutritional Values (Per Serving):

Calories – 237

Fat – 1g

Saturated Fats – 0g

Trans Fats - 0g

Carbohydrates – 23g

Fiber – 6g

Sodium – 396mg

Protein – 9g

Breakfast Casserole

Prep Time: 8-10 min.

Cooking Time: 45 min.

Number of Servings: 4

Freestyle Points per Serving: 4

Ingredients:

- 4 eggs
- 2 teaspoons cinnamon
- 1 cup milk
- 1 1/3 cup egg whites
- 2 apples, peeled and cut to dice
- 8 slices bread, low calorie

Directions:

1. Lightly grease a casserole dish (9x13-inch) with cooking spray. Preheat an oven to 350°F.
2. In a microwave-safe mixing bowl, mix 1 teaspoon cinnamon and apples.
3. Microwave the mix for 2-3 minutes.
4. In the dish, add the bread slices and cooked apples.
5. In a mixing bowl, whisk fresh milk, egg whites, and eggs.
6. Add the mix over the dish; bake for 45 minutes.
7. Serve warm.

Nutritional Values (Per Serving):

Calories – 376

Fat – 9g

Saturated Fats – 3g

Trans Fats - 0g

Carbohydrates – 36g

Fiber – 12g

Sodium – 752mg

Protein – 24g

Bacon Brussels Sprouts

Prep Time: 8-10 min.

Cooking Time: 12-15 min.

Number of Servings: 4

SmartPoints: 1

Ingredients:

- 4 bacon slices, center cut, make small pieces
- 3 shallots, finely diced
- 3 garlic cloves, minced
- 1 pound Brussels sprouts, make halves
- ½ cup water

Directions:

1. Take an Instant Pot; open the top lid.
2. Press "SAUTÉ" cooking function.
3. Coat the pot with some olive oil. In the cooking pot area, add the bacon. Cook until turn crisp for 5-6 minutes.
4. Add in the remaining ingredients; combine well.
5. Close the top lid and make sure the valve is sealed.
6. Press "MANUAL" cooking function. Adjust cooking time to 3-5 minutes.
7. Allow pressure to build and cook the ingredients for the set time.
8. After the set cooking time ends, press "CANCEL" and then press "QPR". Instant Pot will quickly release pressure.
9. Open the top lid, add the cooked mixture in serving plates.
10. Serve warm.

Nutritional Values (Per Serving):

Calories - 176

Fat – 2.5g

Carbohydrates – 34g

Fiber – 7g

Sodium - 144mg

Protein – 13g

Prep Time: 8-10 min.

Cooking Time: 10 min.

Number of Servings: 2

SmartPoints: 1

Ingredients:

- 1 pear, cored and chopped
- 3 tablespoons coconut oil
- 2 tablespoons honey
- 1 plum, stone removed and chopped
- 1 apple, cored and chopped
- ½ teaspoon cinnamon
- 2 tablespoons sunflower seeds, roasted
- ¼ cup pecans, chopped
- ¼ cup coconut, shredded and unsweetened

Directions:

1. Take an Instant Pot; open the top lid.
2. Add the plum with apple, pear, oil, honey, and cinnamon in the cooking pot. Using a spatula, gently stir to combine well.
3. Close the top lid and make sure the valve is sealed.
4. Press "STEAM" cooking function. Adjust cooking time to 10 minutes.
5. Allow pressure to build and cook the ingredients for the set time.
6. After the set cooking time ends, press "CANCEL" and then press "QPR". Instant Pot will quickly release pressure.
7. Open the top lid, set aside the mix.
8. In the pot, mix in the pecans, sunflower seeds, and coconut. Cook on "SAUTE" mode for 4-5 minutes.
9. Add the mix over the fruit mix. Serve warm.

Nutritional Values (Per Serving):

Calories – 137

Fat – 2.5g

Carbohydrates – 5g

Fiber – 3g

Sodium - 74mg

Protein – 4.5g

Prep Time: 8-10 min.

Cooking Time: 10 min.

Number of Servings: 4-6

SmartPoints: 4

Ingredients:

- 7 ounces cheddar cheese, grated
- 1 teaspoon salt
- ½ teaspoon red chili flakes
- 3 large bread rolls
- 4 eggs
- ½ teaspoon sour cream
- 1 tablespoon butter

Directions:

1. Cut the rolls in half. Hollow out the center of each half partially.
2. In a mixing bowl, mix the salt, pepper flakes, and sour cream. Beat the eggs.
3. Add the eggs in bread halves.
4. Take an Instant Pot; open the top lid.
5. Grease the pot with butter and add the bread halves. Top with the spice mix and cheese.
6. Close the top lid and make sure the valve is sealed.
7. Press "STEAM" cooking function. Adjust cooking time to 10 minutes.
8. Allow pressure to build and cook the ingredients for the set time.
9. After the set cooking time ends, press "CANCEL" and then press "QPR". Instant Pot will quickly release pressure.
10. Open the top lid, add the cooked mixture in serving plates.
11. Serve warm.

Nutritional Values (Per Serving):

Calories – 253

Fat – 11.5g

Carbohydrates – 22g

Fiber – 4.5g

Sodium - 87mg

Protein – 15g

Cinnamon Banana Smoothie

Prep Time: 8-10 min.

Cooking Time: 0 min.

Number of Servings: 2

SmartPoints: 6

Ingredients:

- 1 cup low-fat milk
- ½ cup non-fat Greek yogurt
- ¼ teaspoon cinnamon
- 2 dates, pitted, chopped
- 1 ripe banana, peeled, sliced
- 1 tablespoon honey
- Ice cubes as needed

Directions:

1. Add the ingredients one by one in your food processor or blender.
2. Close the lid and blend to make a smooth mix.
3. Add the prepare smoothie in tall serving glasses. Serve chilled.

Nutritional Values (Per Serving):

Calories – 186

Fat – 2.5g

Carbohydrates – 34.5g

Fiber – 4g

Sodium - 26mg

Protein – 5g

Watermelon Chia Smoothie

Prep Time: 8-10 min.

Cooking Time: 0 min.

Number of Servings: 2

SmartPoints: 2

Ingredients:

- 2 slices lemon to garnish
- 1/3 cup water
- 3 cups watermelon cubes, deseeded
- 2 tablespoons chia seeds
- 2 sprigs mint
- Ice cubes as needed

Directions:

1. Add the ingredients one by one in your food processor or blender.
2. Close the lid and blend to make a smooth mix.
3. Add the prepare smoothie in tall serving glasses.
4. Serve chilled. Garnish with mint leaves and a lemon slice.

Nutritional Values (Per Serving):

Calories - 134

Fat – 6g

Carbohydrates – 21.5g

Fiber – 7g

Sodium - 32mg

Protein – 5g

Cucumber Pineapple Smoothie

Prep Time: 8-10 min.

Cooking Time: 0 min.

Number of Servings: 2

SmartPoints: 1

Ingredients:

- 4 cups pineapple cubes, frozen
- 2 bunches flat leaf parsley
- 1 English cucumber, chopped
- 1 ½ cups coconut water
- Juice for 2-3 small lemons
- 8-10 drops stevia

Directions:

1. Add the ingredients one by one in your food processor or blender.
2. Close the lid and blend to make a smooth mix.
3. Add the prepare smoothie in tall serving glasses. Serve chilled.

Nutritional Values (Per Serving):

Calories – 122

Fat – 6g

Carbohydrates – 28g

Sodium – 24mg

Fiber – 5.5g

Protein – 2g

Potato Buttermilk Appetizer

Prep Time: 8-10 min.

Cooking Time: 12 min.

Number of Servings: 6

SmartPoints: 4

Ingredients:

- 1/3 cup buttermilk, low-fat
- ½ teaspoon kosher salt
- ¼ cup sour cream
- 3 cups water
- 2-pound russet potatoes, peeled and make quarters
- 1 teaspoon salt
- 2 tablespoons butter
- Parsley as required, chopped
- Black pepper as needed

Directions:

1. Take an Instant Pot; open the top lid.
2. Add the water, salt, and potato in the cooking pot. Using a spatula, gently stir to combine well.
3. Close the top lid and make sure the valve is sealed.
4. Press "MANUAL" cooking function. Adjust cooking time to 10-12 minutes.
5. Allow pressure to build and cook the ingredients for the set time.
6. After the set cooking time ends, press "CANCEL" and then press "QPR". Instant Pot will quickly release pressure.
7. Open the top lid, drain water except for ½ cup and add the potatoes in a blender. Add ½ cup of water also.
8. Add in the remaining ingredients and blend to create a mash like consistency.
9. Serve warm.

Nutritional Values (Per Serving):

Calories - 138

Fat – 4.5g

Carbohydrates – 26.5g

Fiber – 3g

Sodium - 312mg

Protein – 5g

Orange Glazed Potatoes

Prep Time: 8-10 min.

Cooking Time: 20 min.

Number of Servings: 7-8

SmartPoints: 4

Ingredients:

- 1 tablespoon cinnamon
- 1 tablespoon blackstrap molasses
- ½ cup orange juice
- 4 cups sweet potatoes, make small-sized pieces
- 1 teaspoon vanilla
- ¼ cup sugar

Directions:

1. In a heat-proof bowl, add the potatoes. Mix in the cinnamon, molasses, sugar, orange juice, and vanilla.
2. Take an Instant Pot; open the top lid.
3. Pour 1 cup water and place steamer basket/trivet inside the cooking pot.
4. Arrange the bowl over the basket/trivet.
5. Close the top lid and make sure the valve is sealed.
6. Press "MANUAL" cooking function. Adjust cooking time to 20-22 minutes.
7. Allow pressure to build and cook the ingredients for the set time.
8. After the set cooking time ends, press "CANCEL" and then press "NPR". Instant Pot will slowly and naturally release the pressure for 8-10 minutes.
9. Open the top lid, add the cooked mixture in serving plates.
10. Serve warm.

Nutritional Values (Per Serving):

Calories - 112

Fat – 4.5g

Carbohydrates – 16g

Fiber – 3g

Sodium - 173mg

Protein – 3g

Broccoli Spinach Greens

Prep Time: 8-10 min.

Cooking Time: 5 min.

Number of Servings: 4-5

SmartPoints: 1

Ingredients:

- 2 cups kale, chopped
- 1/2 teaspoon cumin, ground
- 2 cups broccoli, chopped
- 2 cups baby spinach
- 1/2 teaspoon coriander, ground
- 2 cloves garlic, crushed or minced
- 2 tablespoons coconut oil
- 1 tablespoon ginger, minced

Directions:

1. Take an Instant Pot; open the top lid.
2. Press "SAUTÉ" cooking function.
3. In the cooking pot area, add the oil, garlic, ginger, and broccoli. Cook until turn translucent and softened for 4-5 minutes.
4. Add the remaining ingredients.
5. Cook until spinach and kale are wilted.
6. Add the cooked mixture in serving plates.
7. Serve warm.

Nutritional Values (Per Serving):

Calories - 93

Fat – 5.5g

Carbohydrates – 4g

Fiber – 1g

Sodium - 33mg

Protein – 4.5g

Cheesy Artichokes

Prep Time: 8-10 min.

Cooking Time: 12 min.

Number of Servings: 4

SmartPoints: 1

Ingredients:

- 2 teaspoons minced garlic
- 4 washed artichokes, trimmed
- ¼ cup shredded parmesan cheese
- 4 teaspoons olive oil
- ½ cup vegetable broth

Directions:

1. Spread the garlic and oil over the artichokes. Top with the cheese.
2. Take an Instant Pot; open the top lid.
3. Pour the broth and place steamer basket/trivet inside the cooking pot.
4. Arrange the artichokes over the basket/trivet.
5. Close the top lid and make sure the valve is sealed.
6. Press "MANUAL" cooking function. Adjust cooking time to 8-12 minutes. For smaller artichokes, 8 minutes is adequate.
7. Allow pressure to build and cook the ingredients for the set time.
8. After the set cooking time ends, press "CANCEL" and then press "QPR". Instant Pot will quickly release pressure.
9. Open the top lid, add the cooked mixture in serving plates.
10. Serve warm.

Nutritional Values (Per Serving):

Calories – 157

Fat – 3.5g

Carbohydrates – 17.5g

Fiber – 4g

Sodium - 134mg

Protein – 5.5g

Potato Chicken Roast

Prep Time: 8-10 min.

Cooking Time: 20 min.

Number of Servings: 5-6

SmartPoints: 5

Ingredients:

- 2 cloves garlic, minced
- 2 teaspoons fresh thyme
- 1 teaspoon black pepper
- 1 large roasting chicken
- 2 teaspoons extra-virgin olive oil
- 1 teaspoon paprika
- 1 cup baby carrots
- 1 ½ cup water
- 1 teaspoon sea salt
- 2 stalks celery, chopped
- 2 medium potatoes, cubed

Directions:

1. Coat the chicken with the olive oil, garlic, thyme, black pepper, paprika, and salt. Add the celery and carrots inside the chicken cavity.
2. Take an Instant Pot; open the top lid.
3. Add the chicken and water in the cooking pot. Add the potatoes.
4. Close the top lid and make sure the valve is sealed.
5. Press "MANUAL" cooking function. Adjust cooking time to 20 minutes.
6. Allow pressure to build and cook the ingredients for the set time.
7. After the set cooking time ends, press "CANCEL" and then press "NPR". Instant Pot will slowly and naturally release the pressure for 8-10 minutes.
8. Open the top lid, add the cooked mixture in serving plates. Cook on sauté for a few minutes, if you want to thicken the sauce.
9. Serve warm.

Nutritional Values (Per Serving):

Calories – 276

Fat – 2.5g

Carbohydrates – 12g

Fiber – 1g

Sodium - 358mg

Protein – 23.5g

Coconut Curry Chicken

Prep Time: 8-10 min.

Cooking Time: 10 min.

Number of Servings: 5-6

SmartPoints: 7

Ingredients:

- 1 tablespoon curry powder
- 1 teaspoon turmeric
- 1/4 cup lemon juice
- 1 can full-fat coconut milk
- 1/2 teaspoon lemon zest
- 1/2 teaspoon salt
- 4-pounds chicken breast, skin removed

Directions:

1. In a mixing bowl, mix the lemon juice, coconut milk, curry powder, turmeric, lemon zest, and salt.
2. Take an Instant Pot; open the top lid.
3. Add the chicken and bowl mix in the cooking pot. Using a spatula, gently stir to combine well.
4. Close the top lid and make sure the valve is sealed.
5. Press "POULTRY" cooking function with default cooking time.
6. Allow pressure to build and cook the ingredients for the set time.
7. After the set cooking time ends, press "CANCEL" and then press "NPR". Instant Pot will slowly and naturally release the pressure for 8-10 minutes.
8. Open the top lid, add the cooked mixture in serving plates.
9. Serve warm.

Nutritional Values (Per Serving):

Calories – 133

Fat – 11g

Carbohydrates – 8g

Fiber – 1.5g

Sodium - 295mg

Protein – 6.5g

Garlic Salsa Chicken

Prep Time: 8-10 min.

Cooking Time: 25 min.

Number of Servings: 5-6

SmartPoints: 0

Ingredients:

- 1/8 teaspoon oregano
- Salt as needed
- ¼ teaspoon garlic powder
- 1 ½ pound skinless chicken tenders
- 1/8 teaspoon ground cumin
- 16 ounces roasted salsa verde

Directions:

1. Mix the oregano, garlic powder, salt, and cumin in a mixing bowl.
2. Coat the chicken with the prepared mix and set aside for 30 minutes to season.
3. Take an Instant Pot; open the top lid.
4. Add the seasoned chicken and salsa in the cooking pot. Using a spatula, gently stir to combine well.
5. Close the top lid and make sure the valve is sealed.
6. Press "MANUAL" cooking function. Adjust cooking time to 18-20 minutes.
7. Allow pressure to build and cook the ingredients for the set time.
8. After the set cooking time ends, press "CANCEL" and then press "QPR". Instant Pot will quickly release pressure.
9. Open the top lid, shred the chicken; add the cooked mixture in serving plates.
10. Serve warm.

Nutritional Values (Per Serving):

Calories – 153

Fat – 2.5g

Carbohydrates – 6g

Fiber – 2g

Sodium - 421mg

Protein – 26g

Prep Time: 8-10 min.

Cooking Time: 15 min.

Number of Servings: 3-4

SmartPoints: 0

Ingredients:

- ½ cup water or chicken broth
- 4 chicken breasts
- 1 jar salsa
- 1 cup plain, fat-free Greek yogurt

Directions:

1. Take an Instant Pot; open the top lid.
2. Add all the ingredients in the cooking pot. Using a spatula, gently stir to combine well.
3. Close the top lid and make sure the valve is sealed.
4. Press "MANUAL" cooking function. Adjust cooking time to 15 minutes.
5. Allow pressure to build and cook the ingredients for the set time.
6. After the set cooking time ends, press "CANCEL" and then press "NPR". Instant Pot will slowly and naturally release the pressure for 8-10 minutes.
7. Open the top lid, add the cooked mixture in serving plates.
8. Serve warm.

Nutritional Values (Per Serving):

Calories - 314

Fat – 6.5g

Carbohydrates – 31g

Fiber – 3.5g

Sodium - 742mg

Protein – 31g

Cheese Cream Chicken

Prep Time: 8-10 min.

Cooking Time: 25-30 min.

Number of Servings: 6

Freestyle Points per Serving: 5

Ingredients:

- 1 (8-ounce) package biscuits
- 1/3 cup light sour cream
- ¼ cup ranch dressing
- 4 ounce light cream cheese
- 2 cups cooked shredded chicken
- 5 slices bacon, cooked and crumbled
- ½ cup low-fat cheese, shredded

Directions:

1. Preheat an oven to 375°F. Grease a baking pan (9x13) with a cooking spray.
2. Crush the biscuits; arrange over the baking pan.
3. Take a mixing bowl (either medium or large size), add in the cream cheese, sour cream, ranch dressing and chicken in the bowl to mix well with each other.
4. Add the mix over the biscuits and spread evenly.
5. Bake for 30 minutes. Serve warm.

Nutritional Values (Per Serving):

Calories – 263

Fat – 17g

Saturated Fats – 9g

Trans Fats - 0g

Carbohydrates – 18g

Fiber – 1g

Sodium – 742mg

Protein – 11g

Chicken Veggie Rice

Prep Time: 8-10 min.

Cooking Time: 15 min.

Number of Servings: 6

Freestyle Points per Serving: 2

Ingredients:

- 1 onion, chopped
- 2 cloves of garlic, minced
- 1 teaspoon olive oil
- 4 large egg whites
- 12 ounces skinless chicken breasts make ½" cubes
- 2 cups long-grain brown rice, cooked
- 3 tablespoons soy sauce, low-sodium
- ½ cups carrots, chopped
- ½ cup frozen green peas

Directions:

1. Take a skillet or saucepan (medium size preferable); heat it over a medium cooking flame.
2. Add the oil and heat it.
3. Add the egg whites and cook until scrambled. Set it aside.
4. Add and cook the onions, garlic, and chicken breasts for 5-6 minutes until lightly brown. Add the carrots and peas.
5. Cook for 2-3 more minutes.
6. Stir in the rice and soy sauce. Add the cooked egg mix and stir-cook for 2-3 more minutes.
7. Serve warm.

Nutritional Values (Per Serving):

Calories – 142

Fat – 3g

Saturated Fats – 1g

Trans Fats - 0g

Carbohydrates – 21g

Fiber – 2g

Sodium – 642mg

Protein – 23g

Turkey Apple Patties

Prep Time: 8-10 min.

Cooking Time: 10 min.

Number of Servings: 4

Freestyle Points per Serving: 1

Ingredients:

- 1 tablespoon sage, minced
- 2 teaspoons Dijon mustard
- 1 green apple, cored and grated
- 1-pound lean skinless ground turkey
- ½ teaspoon salt
- ¼ teaspoon onion powder
- 2 teaspoons olive oil
- ¼ teaspoon pepper
- ¼ teaspoon garlic powder

Directions:

1. Take a mixing bowl (either medium or large size), add in the ingredients except for the olive oil in the bowl to mix well with each other.
2. Make 4 patties and add in your fridge for 30 minutes before cooking.
3. Take a skillet or saucepan (medium size preferable); heat it over a medium cooking flame.
4. Add the oil and heat it.
5. Cook the patties on both the sides until turning brown for 4-5 minutes.
6. Serve with green veggies or salad mix.

Nutritional Values (Per Serving):

Calories – 137

Fat – 3g

Saturated Fats – 0g

Trans Fats - 0g

Carbohydrates – 25g

Fiber – 4g

Sodium – 37mg

Protein – 6g

Sesame Sherry Chicken

Prep Time: 8-10 min.

Cooking Time: 13 min.

Number of Servings: 3-4

SmartPoints: 4

Ingredients:

- 1 tablespoon low-sodium soy sauce
- 1-pound boneless chicken breast, skin less
- 1 tablespoon maple syrup
- 2 tablespoons raw sesame seeds
- 1 tablespoon water
- ½ teaspoon five-spice powder
- 1 teaspoon ginger root, grated
- 1 tablespoon dry sherry
- Pepper and salt as per taste
- 1 cup water
- 2 tablespoons peanut oil

Directions:

1. Take an Instant Pot; open the top lid.
2. Press "SAUTÉ" cooking function.
3. In the cooking pot area, add and toast the sesame seeds for 3 minutes.
4. In a mixing bowl, combine the water, soy sauce, and maple syrup. Add the ginger, five-spice powder and sherry.
5. In a mixing dish, mix the flour, pepper, and salt. Coat the chicken with the flour mixture.
6. Add the chicken in the pot. Sauté until the sides have browned. Add the soy sauce mixture and add 1 cup water.
7. Close the top lid and make sure the valve is sealed.
8. Press "MANUAL" cooking function. Adjust cooking time to 10 minutes.
9. Allow pressure to build and cook the ingredients for the set time.

10. After the set cooking time ends, press "CANCEL" and then press "NPR". Instant Pot will slowly and naturally release the pressure for 8-10 minutes.
11. Open the top lid, add the cooked mixture in serving plates.
12. Serve warm with peanut oil on top.

Nutritional Values (Per Serving):

Calories - 234

Fat – 8g

Carbohydrates – 5.5g

Fiber – 0g

Sodium - 317mg

Protein – 17.5g

Coconut Chicken Delight

Prep Time: 8-10 min.

Cooking Time: 10 min.

Number of Servings: 2

SmartPoints: 5

Ingredients:

- 1 teaspoon fish sauce
- 1 tbs. olive oil
- 2 cups chicken thighs (skinless and boneless)
- 1 tbs. lime juice
- 1 tbs. coconut milk
- 7-8 fresh mint leaves
- ½ tbs. grated fresh ginger
- Fresh cilantro as needed

Directions:

1. In a mixing bowl (heat-proof), mix all the mentioned ingredients except the chicken.
2. Take an Instant Pot; open the top lid.
3. Add the chicken and bowl mix in the cooking pot. Using a spatula, gently stir to combine well.
4. Close the top lid and make sure the valve is sealed.
5. Press "POULTRY" cooking function. Adjust cooking time to 10 minutes.
6. Allow pressure to build and cook the ingredients for the set time.
7. After the set cooking time ends, press "CANCEL" and then press "QPR". Instant Pot will quickly release pressure.
8. Open the top lid, add the cooked mixture in serving plates.
9. Serve warm.

Nutritional Values (Per Serving):

Calories - 214

Fat – 15g

Carbohydrates – 6g

Fiber – 0.5g

Sodium - 423mg

Protein – 14g

Classic Spiced Chicken

Prep Time: 8-10 min.

Cooking Time: 30 min.

Number of Servings: 5-6

SmartPoints: 0

Ingredients:

- ½ teaspoon dried parsley
- 1 teaspoon onion powder
- 1 teaspoon garlic powder
- 1 ½ pound, raw chicken breast, skinless and boneless
- ½ teaspoon dried oregano
- ½ teaspoon dried basil
- 2 cups chicken broth
- ¼ teaspoon black pepper
- ¼ teaspoon salt

Directions:

1. Add all the spices to season the chicken.
2. Take an Instant Pot; open the top lid.
3. Add the chicken and broth in the cooking pot. Using a spatula, gently stir to combine well.
4. Close the top lid and make sure the valve is sealed.
5. Press "MANUAL" cooking function. Adjust cooking time to 8 minutes.
6. Allow pressure to build and cook the ingredients for the set time.
7. After the set cooking time ends, press "CANCEL" and then press "NPR". Instant Pot will slowly and naturally release the pressure for 8-10 minutes.
8. Open the top lid, shred the chicken and add the cooked mixture in serving plates.
9. Serve warm.

Nutritional Values (Per Serving):

Calories - 163

Fat – 3.5g

Carbohydrates – 2g

Fiber – 0g

Sodium - 412mg

Protein – 26g

Oregano Chicken Strips

Prep Time: 8-10 min.

Cooking Time: 8 min.

Number of Servings: 6-7

SmartPoints: 4

Ingredients:

- 1 teaspoon cayenne pepper
- 1/2 teaspoon cilantro
- 1 cup flour
- 1 teaspoon kosher salt
- 1/2 teaspoon oregano
- 1-pound chicken filet, make strips
- 3 tablespoons sesame oil
- 1/2 teaspoon paprika
- 1/2 cup milk
- 1 teaspoon turmeric

Directions:

1. Add the flour in a mixing bowl. Mix in the salt, cayenne pepper, cilantro, oregano, paprika, and turmeric.
2. Pour the milk in a separate bowl.
3. Dip the chicken strips in the milk; dip them in the flour mixture to coat well.
4. Take an Instant Pot; open the top lid.
5. Press "SAUTÉ" cooking function.
6. In the cooking pot area, add the oil and chicken strips.
7. Cook the chicken strips for 3 minutes on each side.
8. Add the chicken to paper towel; serve warm.

Nutritional Values (Per Serving):

Calories - 207

Fat – 8.5g

Carbohydrates – 16g

Fiber – 2g

Sodium - 243mg

Protein – 17.5g

Soy Turkey Meatballs

Prep Time: 8-10 min.

Cooking Time: 10 min.

Number of Servings: 2-3

SmartPoints: 6

Ingredients:

- 2 saltine crackers, crushed
- 1 ½ tablespoons buttermilk
- ½ pound turkey meat, ground
- ½ tablespoon canola oil
- 2 tablespoons green onion, chopped
- A pinch of salt and black pepper
- ½ tablespoon sesame seeds

For the sauce:

- 2 tablespoon rice vinegar
- 1 teaspoon ginger, grated
- 1 garlic clove, minced
- 4 tablespoons soy sauce
- 1 ½ tablespoon brown sugar
- 1 tablespoon canola oil
- A pinch of black pepper
- ½ tablespoon cornstarch

Directions:

1. In a bowl, mix the turkey, crackers, green onions, salt, pepper, and buttermilk.
2. Prepare 8 meatballs and leave them aside.
3. In another mixing bowl, mix the soy sauce, vinegar, garlic, ginger, canola oil (1 tbs.), brown sugar, black pepper and, cornstarch and stir well.
4. Take an Instant Pot; open the top lid.
5. Press "SAUTÉ" cooking function.
6. In the cooking pot area, add the ½ tbs. oil and heat it.

7. Add the meatballs and brown them for 2 minutes on each side.
8. Add the sauce and stir.
9. Close the top lid and make sure the valve is sealed.
10. Press "MANUAL" cooking function. Adjust cooking time to 10 minutes.
11. Allow pressure to build and cook the ingredients for the set time.
12. After the set cooking time ends, press "CANCEL" and then press "QPR". Instant Pot will quickly release pressure.
13. Open the top lid, add the cooked mixture in serving plates.
14. Serve warm with sesame seeds on top.

Nutritional Values (Per Serving):

Calories - 283

Fat – 4.5g

Carbohydrates – 12g

Fiber – 3g

Sodium - 476mg

Protein – 9g

Orange Pineapple Chicken

Prep Time: 8-10 min.

Cooking Time: 12 min.

Number of Servings: 8

Freestyle Points per Serving: 1

Ingredients:

- ¼ cup soy sauce
- 1 teaspoon garlic powder
- 1-pound skinless chicken breasts, make 2-inch chunks
- ½ cup orange juice
- 1 teaspoon onion powder
- ½ teaspoon ginger
- ½ yellow bell pepper, seeded and cubed
- ½ red bell pepper, seeded and cubed
- 1 teaspoon black pepper
- 1 teaspoon salt
- ½ red onion, make wedges
- 1 ½ cups pineapple, make slices

Directions:

1. Take a mixing bowl (either medium or large size), add in the chicken, orange juice, soy sauce, garlic powder, onion powder, black pepper, salt and ginger in the bowl to mix well with each other.
2. Place to marinate for 2 hours inside the fridge.
3. Take the skewers. Skew the bell pepper, onions, and pineapple, and chicken onto them in altering manner.
4. Heat the grill to high-temperature setting; cook the skewers for 5-6 minutes on each side until cooks well.
5. Serve warm.

Nutritional Values (Per Serving):

Calories – 238

Fat – 1g

Saturated Fats – 0g

Trans Fats - 0g

Carbohydrates – 34g

Fiber – 5g

Sodium – 723mg

Protein – 20g

Prep Time: 8-10 min.

Cooking Time: 15-20 min.

Number of Servings: 5-6

Freestyle Points per Serving: 1

Ingredients:

- 1 teaspoon black pepper
- 1 teaspoon onion powder
- 1-pound ground skinless turkey breasts
- ½ teaspoon salt
- 1 teaspoon garlic powder
- ¼ cup teriyaki sauce
- ¼ cup BBQ sauce, sugar-free
- 1 teaspoon paprika
- 1 teaspoon cumin
- 1/3 cup apple cider vinegar
- 1 tablespoon brown sugar

Directions:

1. Take a mixing bowl (either medium or large size), add in the dry ingredients except for the sugar in the bowl to mix well with each other. Form into 12 meatballs.
2. In another bowl, combine the wet ingredients and sugar.
3. Preheat an oven to 375°F.
4. Bake the meatballs for 8-10 minutes.
5. Turn the meatballs and cook for 10 more minutes.
6. Serve with the sauce mix.

Nutritional Values (Per Serving):

Calories – 281

Fat – 1g

Saturated Fats – 0g

Trans Fats - 0g

Carbohydrates – 43g

Fiber – 6g

Sodium – 532mg

Protein – 16g

Chicken Mushroom Meatballs

Prep Time: 8-10 min.

Cooking Time: 25-30 min.

Number of Servings: 9-10

Freestyle Points per Serving: 5

Ingredients:

- 1/3 cup whole wheat bread crumbs
- ¼ cup pecorino cheese, grated
- 8 ounces cremini mushrooms, chopped finely
- 1-pound lean ground chicken
- 1 large egg, beaten
- 1 teaspoon salt
- 2 tablespoons chopped parsley
- 3 cloves of garlic, minced
- A dash of black pepper
- ½ tablespoon all-purpose flour
- ½ tablespoon unsalted butter
- ¼ cup shallots, chopped
- 1/3 cup Marsala wine
- ¾ cup chicken broth, low sodium
- 3 ounces shiitake mushrooms, make slices

Directions:

1. Preheat an oven to 400°F.
2. Take a mixing bowl (either medium or large size), add in the mushrooms, chicken, bread crumbs, cheese, egg, parsley, garlic, salt, and pepper in the bowl to mix well with each other.
3. Form small meatballs and arrange in a greased baking sheet. Bake for 20 minutes and set aside.
4. Take a mixing bowl (either medium or large size), add in the flour, Marsala wine, and broth in the bowl to mix well with each other.
5. Take a skillet or saucepan (medium size preferable); heat it over a medium cooking flame.

6. Add the butter and heat it.
7. Add and sauté the shallots until fragrant. Stir in the mushrooms and cook for 2-3 minutes.
8. Pour in the broth mix; simmer for 5 minutes until the mix thickens.
9. Serve meatballs with the sauce.

Nutritional Values (Per Serving):

Calories – 82

Fat – 3g

Saturated Fats – 1g

Trans Fats - 0g

Carbohydrates – 6g

Fiber – 1g

Sodium – 423mg

Protein – 5g

Teriyaki Pork Meal

Prep Time: 8-10 min.

Cooking Time: 25 min.

Number of Servings: 5-6

SmartPoints: 6

Ingredients:

- 4 cloves garlic, minced
- ½ large onion, chopped
- 2 tablespoons olive oil
- 2-pounds pork tenderloin, make strips
- 3 red chili pepper, chopped
- 1 cup chicken broth
- ¼ cup brown sugar
- ¼ teaspoon black pepper
- ½ cup teriyaki sauce

Directions:

1. Take an Instant Pot; open the top lid.
2. Press "SAUTÉ" cooking function.
3. In the cooking pot area, add the oil and tenderloins. Stir-cook constantly for 5 minutes or until they become brown.
4. Add in garlic, onion, red chili pepper and black pepper. Add the remaining ingredients.
5. Close the top lid and make sure the valve is sealed.
6. Press "MEAT/STEW" cooking function. Adjust cooking time to 20 minutes.
7. Allow pressure to build and cook the ingredients for the set time.
8. After the set cooking time ends, press "CANCEL" and then press "NPR". Instant Pot will slowly and naturally release the pressure for 8-10 minutes.
9. Open the top lid, add the cooked mixture in serving plates.
10. Serve warm cooked rice (optional).

Nutritional Values (Per Serving):

Calories – 332

Fat – 7g

Carbohydrates – 14.5g

Fiber – 0g

Sodium - 753mg

Protein – 8.5g

Beef Lettuce Burgers

Prep Time: 8-10 min.

Cooking Time: 10 min.

Number of Servings: 4

Freestyle Points per Serving: 4

Ingredients:

- ½ teaspoon salt
- 1 tablespoon Worcestershire sauce
- 2 teaspoons garlic, minced
- ¼ teaspoon pepper
- 4 hamburger buns, low calorie
- 1 pound ground beef
- Shredded lettuce as needed

Directions:

1. Coat a griddle with some olive oil or cooking spray and heat it.
2. Take a mixing bowl (either medium or large size), add in the pepper, salt, Worcestershire sauce, garlic, and beef in the bowl to mix well with each other.
3. Prepare 4 patties from the mix.
4. Place them over the griddle and cook for 4-5 minutes on each side.
5. Take the buns and make burgers with your favorite toppings, lettuce, and serve.

Nutritional Values (Per Serving):

Calories – 327

Fat – 12g

Saturated Fats – 5g

Trans Fats - 0g

Carbohydrates – 22g

Fiber – 1g

Sodium – 642mg

Protein – 27g

Prep Time: 8-10 min.

Cooking Time: 15 min.

Number of Servings: 4

Freestyle Points per Serving: 5

Ingredients:

- 4 pork loin chops, center-cut
- 1/3 cup non-fat, half-and-half
- 1/3 cup fat-free chicken stock
- 1/2 teaspoon salt
- 1 1/2 tablespoon Dijon mustard
- 1/2 teaspoon black pepper
- 1/2 teaspoon onion powder
- Pinch of dried thyme

Directions:

1. Rub the salt, pepper, and onion powder over the chops.
2. Take a skillet or saucepan (medium size preferable); heat it over a medium cooking flame.
3. Add the oil and heat it.
4. Add the meat and cook, while stirring, until turns evenly brown for 3-4 minute per side.
5. Pour the stock, mustard, and half-and-half.
6. Lower temperature setting; cook for 6-7 more minutes.
7. When the sauce becomes thick, add the thyme. Serve warm.

Nutritional Values (Per Serving):

Calories – 134

Fat – 5g

Saturated Fats – 2g

Trans Fats - 0g

Carbohydrates – 2g

Fiber – 0g

Sodium – 447mg

Protein – 14g

Chipotle Beef Roast

Prep Time: 8-10 min.

Cooking Time: 40 min.

Number of Servings: 7-8

SmartPoints: 3

Ingredients:

- 1 tablespoon ground cumin
- 1 lime, juiced
- 1/2 medium onion, chopped
- 5 cloves of garlic, minced
- 4 tablespoons chipotles in adobo sauce
- 1 cup water
- 3-pounds beef eye round roast, fat trimmed
- 1 tablespoon ground oregano
- 1/2 teaspoon ground cloves
- 2 1/2 teaspoon salt
- Black pepper as per taste
- 1 teaspoon oil
- 3 bay leaves

Directions:

1. Add the onion, garlic, cumin, lime juice, chipotles, oregano, and cloves in a blender. Add water and blend until smooth.
2. Season the beef with pepper and salt.
3. Take an Instant Pot; open the top lid.
4. Press "SAUTÉ" cooking function.
5. In the cooking pot area, add the oil and heat it.
6. Add the beef and cook for 5 minutes until it turns brown on all sides. Add the puree and bay leaves.
7. Close the top lid and make sure the valve is sealed.
8. Press "MANUAL" cooking function. Adjust cooking time to 35 minutes.
9. Allow pressure to build and cook the ingredients for the set time.
10. After the set cooking time ends, press "CANCEL" and then press "QPR". Instant Pot will quickly release pressure.

11. Open the top lid, remove the bay leave and shred the meat.
12. Add the cooked mixture in serving plates, adjust seasoning if needed. Serve warm.

Nutritional Values (Per Serving):

Calories - 217

Fat – 5g

Carbohydrates – 9g

Fiber – 1.5g

Sodium - 724mg

Protein – 21g

Corn Potato Beef

Prep Time: 8-10 min.

Cooking Time: 25 min.

Number of Servings: 6-8

SmartPoints: 3

Ingredients:

- 3 cups beef broth
- 1 teaspoon olive oil
- Pepper and salt as needed
- 1-pound lean beef, make cubes
- 1 bay leaf
- ½ teaspoon dried oregano
- 1 onion, chopped
- 1 cup carrots, chopped
- 15-ounces tomato sauce
- 2 garlic cloves, minced
- 1 cup frozen corn, drained
- 1 cup celery, chopped
- 1 ½ cups red potatoes, cubed and skin removed

Directions:

1. Take an Instant Pot; open the top lid.
2. Press "SAUTÉ" cooking function.
3. In the cooking pot area, add the oil, garlic, dried oregano, and onions. Cook until turn translucent and softened for 1-2 minutes.
4. add the meat and cook for about 3–4 minutes to evenly brown.
5. Add the celery, carrots, pepper, and salt; stir-cook for more 3–4 minutes.
6. Add in the remaining ingredients; combine well.
7. Close the top lid and make sure the valve is sealed.
8. Press "MANUAL" cooking function. Adjust cooking time to 15-18 minutes.
9. Allow pressure to build and cook the ingredients for the set time.
10. After the set cooking time ends, press "CANCEL" and then press "NPR". Instant Pot will slowly and naturally release the pressure for 8-10 minutes.
11. Open the top lid, add the cooked mixture in serving plates.

12. Serve warm.

Nutritional Values (Per Serving):

Calories – 346

Fat – 7g

Carbohydrates – 28.5g

Fiber – 6g

Sodium - 546mg

Protein – 21g

Prep Time: 8-10 min.

Cooking Time: 15 min.

Number of Servings: 5-6

SmartPoints: 4

Ingredients:

- 2 white onions, sliced
- 1 cup ground beef
- 3 tablespoons chives
- 8-ounces penne
- 1 teaspoon olive oil
- 1 teaspoon salt
- 2 tablespoons soy sauce
- 1 teaspoon turmeric
- 4 cups chicken stock
- ½ cup tomato sauce
- 1 teaspoon cilantro
- ½ tablespoon paprika

Directions:

1. Take an Instant Pot; open the top lid.
2. Press "SAUTÉ" cooking function.
3. In the cooking pot area, add the oil and onions.
4. Add the ground beef, salt, turmeric, cilantro, and paprika.
5. Stir the mixture well and sauté it for 4 minutes.
6. Remove the mixture from the pot and set aside.
7. In the pot, add the soy sauce, tomato sauce, and chives. Sauté the mixture for 3 minutes.
8. Add the pasta and chicken stock. Mix in the beef mixture.
9. Close the top lid and make sure the valve is sealed.
10. Press "MANUAL" cooking function. Adjust cooking time to 8 minutes.
11. Allow pressure to build and cook the ingredients for the set time.
12. After the set cooking time ends, press "CANCEL" and then press "QPR". Instant Pot will quickly release pressure.

13. Open the top lid, add the cooked mixture in serving plates.
14. Serve warm.

Nutritional Values (Per Serving):

Calories - 243

Fat – 10.5g

Carbohydrates – 21.5g

Fiber – 3g

Sodium - 586mg

Protein – 15g

Classic Oregano Tenderloins

Prep Time: 8-10 min.

Cooking Time: 25 min.

Number of Servings: 6-8

SmartPoints: 1

Ingredients:

- 1 teaspoon onion powder
- 1 teaspoon garlic powder
- 2 teaspoons dried oregano
- 2 teaspoons dried thyme
- 1 teaspoon table salt
- 2 teaspoons olive oil
- 1 teaspoon black pepper
- 2-pounds lean pork tenderloin

Directions:

1. In a mixing bowl, mix together oregano, thyme, onion powder, garlic powder, salt, and pepper.
2. Coat the oil over the pork and sprinkle the herb mixture. Let it rest for 30 minutes to season.
3. Take an Instant Pot; open the top lid.
4. Pour 1 cup water and place steamer basket/trivet inside the cooking pot.
5. Arrange the pork over the basket/trivet.
6. Close the top lid and make sure the valve is sealed.
7. Press "MANUAL" cooking function. Adjust cooking time to 25 minutes.
8. Allow pressure to build and cook the ingredients for the set time.
9. After the set cooking time ends, press "CANCEL" and then press "QPR". Instant Pot will quickly release pressure.
10. Open the top lid, add the cooked mixture in serving plates.
11. Serve warm.

Nutritional Values (Per Serving):

Calories – 267

Fat – 3.5g

Carbohydrates – 38.5g

Fiber – 6g

Sodium - 221mg

Protein – 23.5g

Prep Time: 8-10 min.

Cooking Time: 30 min.

Number of Servings: 5-6

SmartPoints: 5

Ingredients:

- 1 tablespoon chili powder
- 1 1/2 teaspoon ground cumin
- 1/4 teaspoon cayenne pepper
- 1 tablespoon paprika
- 2 tablespoons brown sugar
- 1 teaspoon salt
- 1 pepper, ground as per taste
- 1/4 cup apple cider vinegar
- 2 tablespoon molasses
- 1 1/2-pound pork tenderloin
- 1/3 cup ketchup
- 2 teaspoons Worcestershire sauce

Directions:

1. Prepare the rub by mixing the paprika, brown sugar, chili powder, cumin, cayenne pepper, salt, and black pepper.
2. Rub the spice mix on to the pork. Set aside 30 minutes to season.
3. Take an Instant Pot; open the top lid.
4. Pour 1 cup water and place steamer basket/trivet inside the cooking pot.
5. Arrange the pork over the basket/trivet.
6. Close the top lid and make sure the valve is sealed.
7. Press "MANUAL" cooking function. Adjust cooking time to 30 minutes.
8. Allow pressure to build and cook the ingredients for the set time.
9. After the set cooking time ends, press "CANCEL" and then press "QPR". Instant Pot will quickly release pressure.
10. Open the top lid, add the cooked mixture in serving plates.

11. Mix the remaining ingredients in a bowl and serve the pork with the bowl sauce on top.
12. Serve warm.

Nutritional Values (Per Serving):

Calories - 234

Fat – 3.5g

Carbohydrates – 14.5g

Fiber – 2g

Sodium - 513mg

Protein – 22.5g

Avocado Crab Salad

Prep Time: 8-10 min.

Cooking Time: 0 min.

Number of Servings: 2

Freestyle Points per Serving: 5

Ingredients:

- 2 teaspoons Asian hot sauce
- 1 teaspoon fresh chives
- 2 teaspoons low-fat mayo
- 4-ounce crabmeat, chopped
- 1/4 cup cucumber, diced

For the Avocado:

- 1 small ripe avocado, pitted and sliced
- 2 teaspoon soy sauce
- 1/2 teaspoon sesame seeds

Directions:

1. Take a mixing bowl (either medium or large size), add in the ingredients except for the soy sauce and sesame seeds in the bowl to mix well with each other.
2. Top with the sauce and seeds; serve.

Nutritional Values (Per Serving):

Calories – 178

Fat – 12g

Saturated Fats – 2g

Trans Fats - 0g

Carbohydrates – 11g

Fiber – 5g

Sodium – 563mg

Protein – 13g

Potato Mayo Fish

Prep Time: 8-10 min.

Cooking Time: 12 min.

Number of Servings: 3

Freestyle Points per Serving: 4

Ingredients:

- ½ teaspoon lemon juice
- ½ teaspoon ground mustard
- 3 tablespoons light mayonnaise
- ½ teaspoon pickle relish
- 2 tablespoons green onions, chopped
- Pepper and salt as per taste
- ½ cup butter, melted
- 4 (3-ounce) tilapia fillet
- ½ cup potato flakes

Directions:

1. Preheat an oven to 450°F.
2. Take a mixing bowl (either medium or large size), add in the mayonnaise, pickle, lemon juice, mustard, and green onions in the bowl to mix well with each other.
3. Coat the fish with the mayo mixture and then dredge on the potato flakes; pat gently and sprinkle with pepper and salt as per taste.
4. Arrange over a baking sheet and bake for 12 minutes. After 6 minutes, brush with the butter and cook for 6 more minutes. Serve warm.

Nutritional Values (Per Serving):

Calories – 533

Fat – 32g

Saturated Fats – 18g

Trans Fats - 0g

Carbohydrates – 6g

Fiber – 1g

Sodium – 654mg

Protein – 13g

Tuna Cranberry Salad

Prep Time: 8-10 min.

Cooking Time: 0 min.

Number of Servings: 5

Freestyle Points per Serving: 3

Ingredients:

Seasoning:

- Red pepper flakes, black pepper, sea salt as needed

Salad:

- 3 tablespoons light sour cream
- 1 can (16 ounce) white tuna in spring water
- 3 tables low-fat mayonnaise
- 1/4 cup red onion, minced
- 1 tablespoon lemon juice
- 1 cored apple, sliced
- 1/4 cup dried cranberries
- 1/2 cup celery, chopped

Directions:

1. Take a mixing bowl (either medium or large size), add in the salad ingredients in the bowl to mix well with each other.
2. Season as needed and serve.

Nutritional Values (Per Serving):

Calories – 83

Fat – 1g

Saturated Fats – 0g

Trans Fats - 0g

Carbohydrates – 13g

Fiber – 2g

Sodium – 164mg

Protein – 4g

Banana Mackerel

Prep Time: 8-10 min.

Cooking Time: 28 min.

Number of Servings: 5

SmartPoints: 6

Ingredients:

- 2 tablespoons water
- ¼ cup cream
- 3 peeled bananas, ripe and chopped
- 1 teaspoon brown sugar
- 3 tablespoons oregano
- 1 teaspoon olive oil
- 1-pound mackerel
- 1 teaspoon ground white pepper
- ¼ cup water
- ¼ teaspoon cinnamon

Directions:

1. Sprinkle the bananas with the brown sugar and cream; stir well.
2. Take an Instant Pot; open the top lid.
3. Press "SAUTÉ" cooking function.
4. In the cooking pot area, add the banana mix and sauté for 8 minutes. Stir the bananas frequently.
5. Chop the fish roughly and mix it with the water, ground white pepper, olive oil, and cinnamon.
6. Add in the fish mix and water; combine well.
7. Close the top lid and make sure the valve is sealed.
8. Press "MEAT/STEW" cooking function. Adjust cooking time to 20 minutes.
9. Allow pressure to build and cook the ingredients for the set time.
10. After the set cooking time ends, press "CANCEL" and then press "QPR". Instant Pot will quickly release pressure.
11. Open the top lid, add the cooked mixture in serving plates.

12. Serve warm.

Nutritional Values (Per Serving):

Calories - 196

Fat – 5.5g

Carbohydrates – 18g

Fiber – 2g

Sodium - 152mg

Protein – 21g

Basil Herbed Salmon

Prep Time: 8-10 min.

Cooking Time: 10 min.

Number of Servings: 4

SmartPoints: 1

Ingredients:

- ¼ teaspoon rosemary
- ½ teaspoon dried basil
- 2 tomatoes, chopped
- ½ teaspoon oregano
- 24-ounces wild salmon
- ¼ teaspoon pepper flakes
- 2 tablespoons balsamic vinegar
- ¼ cup basil, chopped
- Pepper and salt as per taste
- 2 teaspoons olive oil
- 1 cup water

Directions:

1. Mix the oregano, basil, pepper flakes, pepper, salt and rosemary in a mixing bowl.
2. Use the mix to season the salmon. Wrap and seal the salmon in a baking sheet.
3. Take an Instant Pot; open the top lid.
4. Pour the water and place steamer basket/trivet inside the cooking pot.
5. Arrange the wrapped salmon over the basket/trivet.
6. Close the top lid and make sure the valve is sealed.
7. Press "MANUAL" cooking function. Adjust cooking time to 8-10 minutes.
8. Allow pressure to build and cook the ingredients for the set time.
9. After the set cooking time ends, press "CANCEL" and then press "QPR". Instant Pot will quickly release pressure.
10. Open the top lid, add the cooked mixture in serving plates.
11. Mix the basil, vinegar, tomatoes, pepper, salt, and olive oil in a bowl. Set aside.
12. Serve warm with the tomato mix.

Nutritional Values (Per Serving):

Calories - 276

Fat – 12.5g

Carbohydrates – 6.5g

Fiber – 2g

Sodium - 83mg

Protein – 36.5g

Rosemary Buttery Fish Meal

Prep Time: 8-10 min.

Cooking Time: 8 min.

Number of Servings: 3-4

SmartPoints: 5

Ingredients:

- 4 tablespoons butter
- 1 teaspoon sea salt
- 1 red chili pepper, seeded and sliced
- 10-ounces anchovies
- ½ teaspoon paprika
- 1 teaspoon dried dill
- 1 teaspoon rosemary
- 1 teaspoon red chili flakes
- 1 tablespoon basil
- ⅓ cup breadcrumbs

Directions:

1. Mix the chili flakes, paprika, sea salt, basil, dry dill, and rosemary together in a bowl.
2. Coat the anchovies with the spice mix.
3. Mix in the chili pepper and let the mixture rest for 10 minutes.
4. Take an Instant Pot; open the top lid.
5. Press "SAUTÉ" cooking function.
6. In the cooking pot area, melt the butter.
7. Dip the spiced anchovies in the breadcrumbs and put in the pot.
8. Cook the anchovies for 4 minutes on each side.
9. Drain on paper towel and serve warm.

Nutritional Values (Per Serving):

Calories - 327

Fat – 24.5g

Carbohydrates – 4.5g

Fiber – 1g

Sodium - 136mg

Protein – 28g

Vegetable Salmon Delight

Prep Time: 8-10 min.

Cooking Time: 10 min.

Number of Servings: 4

SmartPoints: 2

Ingredients:

- 1-pound salmon fillet, skin on
- 1 carrot, julienned
- 1 bell pepper, julienned
- 1 zucchini, julienned
- 1/2 lemon, make slices
- 2 teaspoons olive oil
- 31/2 teaspoon black pepper
- 3/4 cup water
- 1/4 teaspoon salt

Direction:

1. Coat the salmon with the oil and season with pepper and salt.
2. Take an Instant Pot; open the top lid.
3. Pour the water and place steamer basket/trivet inside the cooking pot.
4. Arrange the salmon over the basket/trivet.
5. Close the top lid and make sure the valve is sealed.
6. Press "MANUAL" cooking function. Adjust cooking time to 3 minutes.
7. Allow pressure to build and cook the ingredients for the set time.
8. After the set cooking time ends, press "CANCEL" and then press "QPR". Instant Pot will quickly release pressure.
9. Open the top lid, take out the steamer rack and set aside the cooked salmon.
10. Press "SAUTÉ" cooking function.
11. In the cooking pot area, add the oil and vegetables. Cook until turn softened for 2 minutes.
12. Serve the salmon with sautéed vegetables.

Nutritional Values (Per Serving):

Calories - 207

Fat – 6.5g

Carbohydrates – 8g

Fiber – 1g

Sodium - 183mg

Protein – 23g

Wine Marinates Shrimps

Prep Time: 8-10 min.

Cooking Time: 7 min.

Number of Servings: 3

SmartPoints: 5

Ingredients:

- 1 tablespoon lemon juice
- ½ teaspoon lemon zest
- 2 tablespoons cilantro
- 2 tablespoons apple cider vinegar
- ½ tablespoon salt
- ½ teaspoon ground ginger
- 1 tablespoon olive oil
- ¼ cup white wine
- 1 teaspoon brown sugar
- ½ tablespoon minced garlic
- 1 teaspoon nutmeg
- 1 cup water
- 5 ½ pound peeled shrimps, deveined
- 1 cup parsley

Directions:

1. Chop the cilantro and parsley. Mix the lemon juice, vinegar, lemon zest, salt, white wine, and sugar together in a mixing bowl.
2. Stir the mixture until sugar and salt dissolve completely.
3. Mix the shrimps in the lemon juice mixture. Add the cilantro and parsley and stir well.
4. Mix in the ginger, olive oil, nutmeg, and water. Allow marinating for 15 minutes.
5. Take an Instant Pot; open the top lid.
6. Add the shrimp mix in the cooking pot. Using a spatula, gently stir to combine well.
7. Close the top lid and make sure the valve is sealed.
8. Press "MANUAL" cooking function. Adjust cooking time to 8 minutes.

9. Allow pressure to build and cook the ingredients for the set time.
10. After the set cooking time ends, press "CANCEL" and then press "QPR". Instant Pot will quickly release pressure.
11. Open the top lid, add the cooked mixture in serving plates.
12. Serve warm.

Nutritional Values (Per Serving):

Calories – 153

Fat – 6.5g

Carbohydrates – 8g

Fiber – 2.5g

Sodium - 413mg

Protein – 16g

Bean Shrimp Rice Meal

Prep Time: 8-10 min.

Cooking Time: 25 min.

Number of Servings: 4

SmartPoints: 1

Ingredients:

- 1 ½ cups, low sodium vegetable broth
- 2 tablespoon minced garlic
- 1 cup rice
- ¼ cup butter
- 1 pound, cooked shrimp
- 1 can black beans, rinsed and drained
- Dried cilantro as required

Directions:

1. Take an Instant Pot; open the top lid.
2. Press "SAUTÉ" cooking function.
3. In the cooking pot area, add the butter and rice.
4. Cook for about 2-3 minutes or until it gets a brown texture.
5. Mix in the pepper, garlic, and salt and stir cook for further 2 minutes.
6. Mix in the shrimps, black beans, and broth.
7. Close the top lid and make sure the valve is sealed.
8. Press "MANUAL" cooking function. Adjust cooking time to 4-5 minutes.
9. Allow pressure to build and cook the ingredients for the set time.
10. After the set cooking time ends, press "CANCEL" and then press "NPR". Instant Pot will slowly and naturally release the pressure for 8-10 minutes.
11. Open the top lid, add the cooked mixture in serving plates.
12. Serve warm with cilantro on top.

Nutritional Values (Per Serving):

Calories - 276

Fat – 11.5g

Carbohydrates – 31g

Fiber – 4g

Sodium - 623mg

Protein – 32.5g

Vietnamese Chicken Soup

Prep Time: 8-10 min.

Cooking Time: 40 min.

Number of Servings: 2-3

SmartPoints: 8

Ingredients:

- 1 small onion, make quarters
- ½ tablespoon coriander seeds, toasted
- 1-pound chicken pieces, bone in and skin on
- A small ginger piece, grated
- ½ teaspoon cardamom pods
- ½ lemongrass stalk, chopped
- ½ cinnamon stick
- ½ cardamom pods
- 2 cloves
- 2 tablespoons fish sauce
- ½ bok choy, chopped
- ½ daikon root, spiralized
- 1 tablespoon green onions, chopped

Directions:

1. Take an Instant Pot; open the top lid.
2. Add the chicken with ginger, onion, coriander seeds, cardamom, cloves, lemongrass, fish sauce, daikon, bok choy and water in the cooking pot. Using a spatula, gently stir to combine well.
3. Close the top lid and make sure the valve is sealed.
4. Press "MANUAL" cooking function. Adjust cooking time to 30 minutes.
5. Allow pressure to build and cook the ingredients for the set time.
6. After the set cooking time ends, press "CANCEL" and then press "QPR". Instant Pot will quickly release pressure.
7. Open the top lid, shred the chicken, add the cooked mixture in serving plates.

8. Serve warm with onions on top.

Nutritional Values (Per Serving):

Calories - 176

Fat – 3g

Carbohydrates – 7g

Fiber – 3g

Sodium - 304mg

Protein – 9g

Chicken Corn Spinach Soup

Prep Time: 8-10 min.

Cooking Time: 70-80 min.

Number of Servings: 8

Freestyle Points per Serving: 3

Ingredients:

- 4 cups baby spinach
- 1 white onion, cut to dice
- 3 cloves minced roasted garlic
- 1 pound boneless skinless chicken breasts, roasted and shredded
- 2 cups frozen corn, thawed
- 1 yellow bell pepper, cut to dice
- 3 cups chicken broth, low-sodium
- 1 tablespoon cumin
- 1 tablespoon salt
- 3 poblano peppers, roasted and cut to dice
- 5 cups water
- 1 teaspoon black pepper
- 1 cup fat-free sour cream

Directions:

1. Take a cooking pot or deep saucepan (medium size preferable); heat it over a medium cooking flame.
2. Combine all Ingredients, except for the sour cream in the pot. Mix until well-combined.
3. Boil the mix; let the mix simmer for about 60 minutes (stir in between).
4. Mix in the cream and continue cooking for 10 minutes.
5. Serve warm.

Nutritional Values (Per Serving):

Calories - 141

Fat – 3g

Saturated Fats – 0g

Trans Fats - 0g

Carbohydrates – 14g

Fiber – 2g

Sodium – 194mg

Protein – 15g

Tomato Herb Soup

Prep Time: 8-10 min.

Cooking Time: 15 min.

Number of Servings: 4

Freestyle Points per Serving: 5

Ingredients:

- ½ cup chop into small pieces, onions
- 1 stalk celery, chop into small pieces
- 3 tablespoons olive oil
- 2 cloves of garlic, minced
- 1 cup chicken broth, fat-free and low-sodium
- 1 cup skim milk
- 5 fresh basil leaves
- 1 14-ounce can tomato puree
- Pepper and salt as per taste
- 1 tablespoon cornstarch + 2 tablespoons water

Directions:

1. Mix the cornstarch with water in a bowl.
2. Add the onions and celery in a food processor and pulse until smooth.
3. Take a skillet or saucepan (medium size preferable); heat it over a medium cooking flame.
4. Add the oil and heat it.
5. Add the onion puree. Stir-cook for 3 minutes until translucent.
6. Add the garlic, broth, and tomato puree.
7. Season as per taste. Boil and simmer for 5 minutes.
8. Whisk in the milk, basil leaves, and cornstarch slurry; simmer for another 5 minutes.
9. Serve warm.

Nutritional Values (Per Serving):

Calories – 164

Fat – 10g

Saturated Fats – 1g

Trans Fats - 0g

Carbohydrates – 13g

Fiber – 2g

Sodium – 62mg

Protein – 5g

Chicken Bean Soup

Prep Time: 8-10 min.

Cooking Time: 8 min.

Number of Servings: 3-4

SmartPoints: 0

Ingredients:

- 1 (15.5 oz.) can light kidney beans, drained
- 1 8 oz. can tomato sauce
- 1 small chopped onion
- 1 (15.5 oz.) can seasoned black beans, drained
- 10 oz. frozen corn
- 1 teaspoon cumin
- 1 teaspoon chili powder
- 2 10 oz. cans diced tomatoes with green chilis
- 1 packet taco seasoning
- 2 boneless, skinless chicken breast
- ½ cup water

Directions:

1. Take an Instant Pot; open the top lid.
2. Add the ingredients to the cooking pot. Using a spatula, gently stir to combine well.
3. Close the top lid and make sure the valve is sealed.
4. Press "MANUAL" cooking function. Adjust cooking time to 8 minutes.
5. Allow pressure to build and cook the ingredients for the set time.
6. After the set cooking time ends, press "CANCEL" and then press "NPR". Instant Pot will slowly and naturally release the pressure for 8-10 minutes.
7. Open the top lid, shred the meat, add the cooked mixture in serving plates.
8. Serve warm.

Nutritional Values (Per Serving):

Calories – 462

Fat – 6g

Carbohydrates – 43.5g

Fiber – 12.5g

Sodium - 823mg

Protein – 39g

Mixed Bean Chicken Stew

Prep Time: 8-10 min.

Cooking Time: 10 min.

Number of Servings: 6

SmartPoints: 0

Ingredients:

- 1 ½ pounds chicken breast, skinless and boneless
- 15 oz. black beans
- 15 oz. corn
- 30 oz. great northern beans, rinsed
- 15 oz. kidney beans, rinsed
- 1 ½ cups diced celery stalks
- 1 tablespoon crushed red pepper
- 2 teaspoons garlic powder
- ½ cup chopped onions
- 3 cups water
- 2 teaspoons chili powder
- ½ teaspoon cumin

Directions:

1. Take an Instant Pot; open the top lid.
2. Press "SAUTÉ" cooking function.
3. Coat the pot with cooking spray. In the cooking pot area, add the celery and onions. Cook until turn translucent and softened for 1-2 minutes.
4. Add the beans, corn, water, and spices. Stir well and place the chicken on top.
5. Close the top lid and make sure the valve is sealed.
6. Press "MANUAL" cooking function. Adjust cooking time to 10 minutes.
7. Allow pressure to build and cook the ingredients for the set time.
8. After the set cooking time ends, press "CANCEL" and then press "NPR". Instant Pot will slowly and naturally release the pressure for 8-10 minutes.
9. Open the top lid, shred the meat; add the cooked mixture in serving plates.
10. Serve warm.

Nutritional Values (Per Serving):

Calories - 304

Fat – 3.5g

Carbohydrates – 37.5g

Fiber – 9g

Sodium - 356mg

Protein – 17g

Prep Time: 8-10 min.

Cooking Time: 40 min.

Number of Servings: 2-3

SmartPoints: 2

Ingredients:

- 1 red bell pepper, chopped
- 3-ounces tomatoes, chopped
- 1 small yellow onion, chopped
- 1 green bell pepper, chopped
- 1 celery stalk, chopped
- 1/3 teaspoon hot sauce
- ½ tablespoon chili powder
- ½ pound black beans
- A pinch of salt and black pepper
- 1 teaspoon paprika
- ½ tablespoon cumin
- 1 bay leaf
- 2 cups veggie stock

Directions:

1. Take an Instant Pot; open the top lid.
2. Add the onion with red bell pepper, green bell pepper, tomatoes, celery, black beans, salt, pepper, hot sauce, chili powder, cumin, paprika, bay leaf and stock in the cooking pot. Using a spatula, gently stir to combine well.
3. Close the top lid and make sure the valve is sealed.
4. Press "MANUAL" cooking function. Adjust cooking time to 40 minutes.
5. Allow pressure to build and cook the ingredients for the set time.
6. After the set cooking time ends, press "CANCEL" and then press "QPR". Instant Pot will quickly release pressure.
7. Open the top lid, add the cooked mixture in serving plates.
8. Serve warm.

Nutritional Values (Per Serving):

Calories – 286

Fat – 3g

Carbohydrates – 27.5g

Fiber – 12g

Sodium - 646mg

Protein – 8.5g

Turkey Bean Soup

Prep Time: 8-10 min.

Cooking Time: 20 min.

Number of Servings: 5-6

SmartPoints: 3

Ingredients:

- 15 oz. tomatoes, diced
- 15 oz. red kidney beans, rinsed
- 1 cup red bell pepper, chopped
- ¼ teaspoon salt
- 1-pound turkey, lean ground
- 1 cup onion, diced
- ¼ teaspoon black pepper
- 2 tablespoons chipotle peppers, canned, chopped
- 1 cup crushed tomatoes
- 1 teaspoon chili powder
- 2 teaspoons garlic, make pieces
- 1 teaspoon ground cumin
- Lime wedges and radish slices to serve

Directions:

1. Season the turkey with pepper and salt.
2. Take an Instant Pot; open the top lid.
3. Press "SAUTÉ" cooking function.
4. Coat the pot with cooking oil. In the cooking pot area, add the turkey and cook to evenly brown.
5. Add in the other ingredients; combine well.
6. Close the top lid and make sure the valve is sealed.
7. Press "MANUAL" cooking function. Adjust cooking time to 10 minutes.
8. Allow pressure to build and cook the ingredients for the set time.
9. After the set cooking time ends, press "CANCEL" and then press "QPR". Instant Pot will quickly release pressure.
10. Open the top lid, add the cooked mixture in serving plates.
11. Serve with the lime wedges and radish slices.

Nutritional Values (Per Serving):

Calories - 233

Fat – 5.5g

Carbohydrates – 7g

Fiber – 1.5g

Sodium - 527mg

Protein – 21g

Mushroom Steak Soup

Prep Time: 8-10 min.

Cooking Time: 15 min.

Number of Servings: 4

SmartPoints: 5

Ingredients:

- 1 cup crushed tomatoes
- 1 cup diced carrots
- 1 pound diced steak, fat trimmed
- 1 (8-oz) pack of sliced mushrooms
- 1 cup diced celery stalk
- 2 cups beef stock
- 2 cups water
- 1 cup sliced bell peppers
- ¾ cup diced onion
- 2 tablespoons garlic powder
- 2 teaspoons oregano
- 1 teaspoon thyme
- 1 bay leaf
- Salt as per taste

Directions:

1. Take an Instant Pot; open the top lid.
2. Press "SAUTÉ" cooking function.
3. Coat the pot with cooking spray. In the cooking pot area, add the beef and cook until brown.
4. Mix in the mushrooms, onions, carrots, celery, pepper, and cook until softened.
5. Mix in the water, stock, thyme, oregano, bay leaf, and salt.
6. Close the top lid and make sure the valve is sealed.
7. Press "SOUP" cooking function. Adjust cooking time to 15 minutes.
8. Allow pressure to build and cook the ingredients for the set time.
9. After the set cooking time ends, press "CANCEL" and then press "NPR". Instant Pot will slowly and naturally release the pressure for 8-10 minutes.
10. Open the top lid, add the cooked mixture in serving plates.

11. Serve warm.

Nutritional Values (Per Serving):

Calories – 483

Fat – 17g

Carbohydrates – 15.5g

Fiber – 3g

Sodium - 548mg

Protein – 21g

Made in the USA
Middletown, DE
07 December 2019